Building a Sustainable Supply Chain

Gareth Kane

Terra Infirma Ltd

gareth@terrainfirma.co.uk

First published in 2013 by Dō Sustainability

87 Lonsdale Road, Oxford OX2 7ET, UK

ISBN 978-1-909293-79-3 (eBook-ePub)

ISBN 978-1-909293-80-9 (eBook-PDF)

ISBN 978-1-909293-78-6 (Paperback)

A catalogue record for this title is available from the British Library.

Dō Sustainability strives for net positive social and environmental impact. See our sustainability policy at **www.dosustainability.com**.

Page design and typesetting by Alison Rayner

Cover by Becky Chilcott

For further information on Dō Sustainability, visit our website: **www.dosustainability.com**

DōShorts

Dō Sustainability is the publisher of **DōShorts**: short, high-value ebooks that distil sustainability best practice and business insights for busy, results-driven professionals. Each DōShort can be read in 90 minutes.

New and forthcoming DōShorts – stay up to date

We publish 3 to 5 new DōShorts each month. The best way to keep up to date? Sign up to our short, monthly newsletter. Go to **www. dosustainability.com/newsletter** to sign up to the Dō Newsletter. Some of our latest and forthcoming titles include:

- *How Gamification Can Help Your Business Engage in Sustainability*   Paula Owen
- *Sustainable Energy Options for Business*   Philip Wolfe
- *Adapting to Climate Change: 2.0 Enterprise Risk Management*   Mark Trexler & Laura Kosloff
- *How to Engage Youth to Drive Corporate Responsbility: Roles and Interventions*   Nicolò Wojewoda
- *The Short Guide to Sustainable Investing*   Cary Krosinsky
- *Strategic Sustainability: Why it Matters to Your Business and How to Make it Happen*   Alexandra McKay
- *Sustainability Decoded: How to Unlock Profit Through the Value Chain*   Laura Musikanski
- *Working Collaboratively: A Practical Guide to Achieving More*   Penny Walker
- *Understanding G4: The Concise Guide to Next Generation Sustainability Reporting*   Elaine Cohen

- *Leading Sustainable Innovation*   Nick Coad & Paul Pritchard
- *Leadership for Sustainability and Change*   Cynthia Scott & Tammy Esteves
- *The Social Licence to Operate: Your Management Framework for Complex Times*   Leeora Black

Subscriptions

In addition to individual sales of our ebooks, we now offer subscriptions. Access 60+ ebooks for the price of 5 with a personal subscription to our full e-library. Institutional subscriptions are also available for your staff or students. Visit **www.dosustainability.com/books/subscriptions** or email **veruschka@dosustainability.com**

Write for us, or suggest a DōShort

Please visit **www.dosustainability.com** for our full publishing programme. If you don't find what you need, write for us! Or suggest a DōShort on our website. We look forward to hearing from you.

Abstract

THE MASSIVE OIL SPILL in the Gulf of Mexico in 2010 was not caused by BP, but by a contractor, yet BP got the blame. The toxic waste from the production of Apple products dumped in China in 2011 was not dumped by Apple, but by a supplier, yet Apple got the blame. The horsemeat found in beef burgers in 2013 was not added by Tesco, but by a supplier, yet Tesco got the blame. In all three cases, blame for the damage caused by suppliers floated up through the supply chain until it lodged with the big brand at the top. No longer can companies constrain their corporate responsibility within the factory fence, as that boundary is not recognised by outside observers. This situation is exacerbated by the fact that the majority of most organisations' environmental footprint lies in their supply chain. This means that, to address the sustainability agenda in a meaningful way, they *must* tackle the impacts of their suppliers. Unfortunately, this is a huge challenge as visibility and influence diminishes quickly as you start to work your way down through the layers of suppliers. This book gives a quick but comprehensive guide to the most effective techniques to help you proactively address environmental risks in the supply chain. It covers the following:

- The business case for a sustainable supply chain;

- Supply chains and sustainability: the big picture;

- Making supply chains sustainable: the fundamentals;

- Basic techniques: the 'hard yards' of green procurement;

ABSTRACT

- Intermediate techniques: those requiring changes to operations and products/services;

- Advanced techniques: changes to the business model and corporate philosophy.

The book draws upon exclusive interviews with top sustainability practitioners along with the practical experiences of the author to provide real world examples at the cutting edge.

....

About the Author

 **GARETH KANE** is one of the UK's leading sustainability practitioners, specialising in embedding sustainability into organisations. His consultancy, Terra Infirma Ltd, has attracted a long list of blue-chip clients such as the BBC, BAE Systems plc, Johnson Matthey plc, Viridor, News International (now News UK) and the NHS. He runs the Corporate Sustainability Mastermind Group – a small gathering of top sustainability executives which meets quarterly to discuss sustainability issues and share best practice.

Gareth authored the books *The Three Secrets of Green Business* and *The Green Executive: Corporate Leadership for a Low Carbon Economy*, and he created the 'Green Jujitsu' approach to embedding sustainability into organisations – the subject of another Dō Short of that name.

All the very best,

Gareth.

Acknowledgments

FIRST OF ALL, I must thank all those who contributed their time and expertise in the form of interviews for this book: Tracy Rawling Church, Head of CSR at Kyocera Document Solutions UK; Stephen Weldon, CSR Manager at Greggs plc; Tom Smith, Head of Marketing and Business Development at Sedex; Sean Axon, Group Sustainability Director at Johnson Matthey plc; Ramon Arratia, Sustainability Director at Interface EMEAI; Peter Laybourn, Chief Executive of International Synergies Ltd; and Dan O'Connor, founder of WARP-It. I have also borrowed from interviews for my book *The Green Executive* so I must thank Glen Bennett of EAE Ltd, Martin Blake then of Royal Mail, Nigel Stansfield of InterfaceFLOR and Richard Gillies of Marks & Spencer as I have recycled some of their wisdom. Thanks must also go to my consultancy clients and Corporate Sustainability Mastermind Group members for sharing insights; the latter contributions must remain anonymous under group rules.

Second, I'd like to thank the team at Dō Sustainability for commissioning this book, in particular Nick Bellorini for tapping me up and, in anticipation, Gudrun Freese who will no doubt have had a hand in you getting to hear about it.

And last but not least, I'd like to thank my family: Karen and the Kane boys, Harry, Jimmy and Charlie, for keeping me sane and reminding me why I'm doing this – to help create a better future for the next generation.

....

Contents

CONTENTS

CONTENTS

Introduction

WE GOT OFF THE COACH like a group of tourists, stretched our muscles and plodded up what looked like a sand dune after our spritely guide. We caught up with him at the top of the ridge and looked across a vast lake in the middle of a bowl of sand. Huge gun-like mechanisms on tripods, straight off the set of Star Wars, squirting murky liquid down the slopes, were the only evidence we weren't on a beach. We couldn't see a single living thing; our little group was quite alone.

This dystopian scene was the Brakpan gold tailings deposition site outside Johannesburg, South Africa – the largest of its kind in the world and certainly the largest waste dump I have ever witnessed. We were 100 m above ground level and the waste materials spread for five kilometres ahead of us. Beneath our feet was 378 million tonnes of reprocessed gold mining waste.

Traditionally, South African 'slimes dams' were created right next to gold mines, leading to groundwater pollution and serious health risks to neighbouring communities. In 1978, DRDGold started sluicing down some of these dams with jets of water, pumping the material out of the Johannesburg sprawl, processing it with cyanide to extract more gold, and dumping it on this much better engineered dam. When our guide explained all this, especially the bit about the cyanide, I started to feel rather nervous about being there.

For every 5 tonnes of material processed, the company extracted 1 g of gold, he told us. If you have a 10 g wedding ring on your finger, 50 tonnes of this stuff – the weight of 35 Volkswagen Golf cars – would have to be collected, pumped, processed, re-pumped and dumped to produce the gold to make it. Lots of people wear gold rings, but very few have seen a tailings site like Brakpan.

This is the one of the intractable problems of our globalised world. The most ecologically damaging industries – mining, forestry, farming and the initial processing of their products – are furthest from the average citizen, consumer and/or voter. If you buy a pair of leather shoes, there's nothing on the box to describe the farm, the slaughterhouse or the tannery that was required to deliver up that leather to the shoe producer. Only their nearest neighbours bear witness to the impacts.

Environmental pressure groups, however, have been quite successful at linking the damage at the coal face (metaphorical or actual) to the household brands that people consume. Greenpeace's 2005 campaign targeting 'iWaste' from Apple's product suppliers produced a rare U-turn from the notoriously intransigent Steve Jobs, who jumped from nonchalance to meaningful action in just a few months when he realised the damage the campaign could do for the hip image of his company.[1]

It's not just Apple – many, if not most, corporations are fast coming to the conclusion that they need to do something about the environmental impact of their supply chain. It is no longer possible to simply draw a limit of responsibility around the office building or the factory fence, as outsiders, including customers, do not recognise that boundary. To help you on this journey we're going to look at the why, what and how of creating a more sustainable supply chain.

Note: everybody has a different definition of the word 'sustainability'. In this Dō Short, we are focussing primarily on environmental sustainability, which we will define in Chapter 2.

....

CHAPTER 1

The Business Case for a Sustainable Supply Chain

BEFORE STARTING WORK ON BUILDING a sustainable supply chain, it is vital that you understand the business case for doing so *as it applies to your business*. A chemical company faces quite different drivers for sustainability than, say, a public transport provider, as they have different supply chains, different customers and come under different legislation. Those different drivers will shape quite different supply chain strategies.

In generic terms, the drivers affecting business are:

- legislation and standards;

- cost pressures;

- availability of materials/continuity of supply;

- environmental risk reduction;

- reputational damage;

- customer demand;

- the moral imperative.

Legislation and standards

Years ago, I was at an eco-design conference and got into a conversation with a researcher from an American electronics brand. She was presenting how her company was meeting the EU's then forthcoming Waste Electrical and Electronic Equipment (WEEE) and Restrictions on Hazardous Substances (RoHS) directives. 'Why would a US company care about EU legislation?' I asked naively. 'Because Europe is a huge market,' she answered, 'and we want to be in it.' This exchange brought it home to me that, in a globalised world, legislation can have impacts far beyond its geographical scope as it travels down the supply chain.

Environmentally damaging substances are always at risk from legislation. The Montreal Protocol led to the phasing out of many ozone-depleting substances; the International Maritime Organisation has banned the use of tributyltin-based boat anti-foulings; and the Stockholm Convention on Persistent Organic Pollutants is phasing out or restricting a significant number of pesticides, flame retardants and other chemicals. If such chemicals feature in your supply chain, then the risk of them disappearing must be factored into your forward plans.

Legislation impacts can be wider than just bans, but can include mandatory disclosures. The new UK Government requirement on FTSE companies on carbon reporting is initially restricted to emissions from fossil fuels,[2] emissions from processes and those associated with electricity used on-site (Scope 1 and 2 in the jargon – see Chapter 2). The government has made it clear that it expects that supply chain emissions (Scope 3) will be included in the future.

At the time of writing, the most popular environmental management standard, ISO 14001, is under revision and, when the new version is published in 2015, it is expected to take a lifecycle perspective rather than its current organisational focus. This means that organisations will need to cover issues arising in the supply chain if they wish to retain certification.

Cost pressures

FIGURE 1. Brent oil prices.[3]

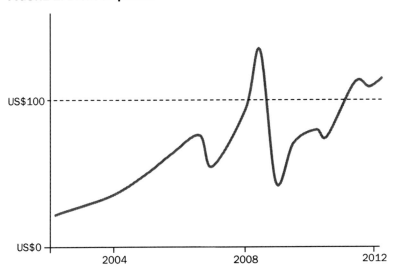

It is common for energy prices to surge ahead of a major recession, but just before the 2007/08 recession they hit record levels (Figure 1). Usually the price will fall again after a crunch, but in 2009 oil prices bounced back and have stayed high since, despite ongoing financial problems in major markets and the shale gas boom in the US. This suggests that the days of cheap oil, upon which the modern economy was built, are over. This impacts not only on road fuel, but also on oil-based polymers, food and many other goods and has been blamed for continuing economic stagnation in major economies.[4]

FIGURE 2. MGI Commodity Index.[5]

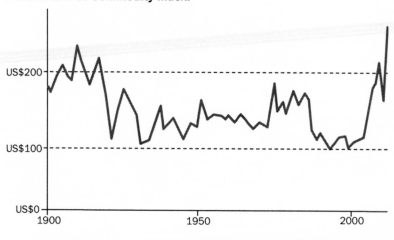

It's not just oil either as you can see from the commodity price index shown in Figure 2. Having spent the twentieth century falling, commodity prices as a whole have bounced back to record levels. It is no surprise then that nearly a third of profit warnings by FTSE 350 companies in 2011 were attributed to rising resource prices.[6]

Availability of resources/security of supply

Rising costs may be the symptom of under-pressure resources, but the ultimate risk is vital materials becoming unavailable. The term 'peak oil' was coined by Hubbert King in the 1950s to describe the situation where supply couldn't keep up with demand (not 'oil running out' as it is often misrepresented). Fatih Birol, Chief Economist at the International Energy

Agency, believes we are now in, or close to, the 'peak zone'.[7] As well as oil, 'peak' has been applied to all sorts of important resources from fish to uranium.

The supply of rare earth materials, essential to many modern electronic gadgets, is of particular concern. It is rumoured that one of the reasons why so many electronic companies have outsourced their production to China is not just to exploit cheap labour but also to ensure access to vital rare earth metals of which China has a fiercely guarded near monopoly (97% of supply[8]).

A recent survey by the manufacturers' organisation EEF found 80% of senior manufacturing executives thought limited access to raw materials was already a business risk. For one in three it was their top risk.[9] As well as physical availability of materials there is also the risk that, say, a particular chemical critical to your operations is either banned or withdrawn voluntarily on environmental grounds. 'Security of supply is part of the business case for us', says Sean Axon of precious metal and catalyst giant Johnson Matthey plc. 'Anticipating and planning for changes in the supply of materials has an impact on the products we make and their formulation.' Despite being in a very different industry, Stephen Weldon of high street bakers Greggs concurs: 'Security of supply is a big issue when we come to negotiate contracts.'

Environmental risk reduction

If you phase out the purchasing of toxic materials, then you won't have to store them on site, which reduces the risk of a major pollution accident. It also contributes to occupational health objectives by reducing the risk to employees at source.

Likewise if you phase out the use of toxic materials in your product, it reduces the risk of, say, being prosecuted for the impacts of that substance. In both these cases, risks are eliminated if the substances never cross into the company premises in the first place.

Reputational damage

In the Introduction, we discussed how Apple was targeted by Greenpeace in 2005. This was not the end of their woes. In 2011, the Beijing-based Institute of Public and Environmental Affairs claimed Apple's Chinese suppliers frequently fail to properly dispose of hazardous waste. 'Apple has made this commitment that it's a green company,' said Ma Jun, the director of the Institute. 'So how do you fulfil your commitment if you don't consider you have responsibility in your suppliers' pollution?' [10]

Note that the NGO does not attack, or even name, the suppliers themselves, or indeed the multitude of other Western brands that use the same suppliers. They pick Apple because its high profile means they will get the headline. This is known as 'tall poppy' syndrome – that the highest profile brand will get targeted because they stand out, and it means it is the biggest names that will be held responsible for the sins of their suppliers. So building a sustainable supply chain is an essential element of brand protection.

As we discussed before, BP and Tesco have also suffered serious reputational damage recently as a result of the actions of their suppliers – in the Gulf of Mexico oil spill and the 'horse-burger' scandal, respectively.

Customer demand

In the same way that reputational damage moves up the value chain to your organisation, it can also flow through to your customers. It is becoming increasingly common that customers are demanding that first-tier suppliers take responsibility for lower tier suppliers. 'Some of the surveys and questionnaires we receive from customers almost take it as read that the company is doing everything we should within its own operational boundary', says Johnson Matthey's Sean Axon. 'They are now much more interested in our management of our suppliers.'

There is also the risk that a rival or newcomer will make your product/service redundant by replacing it with a more sustainable equivalent. For example, the rise of biodiesel production means that most glycerol in the UK now comes from biodiesel by-products, dominating the market over traditional fossil fuel sources.[11] Or as Ramon Arratia of flooring company InterfaceFLOR put it, 'we are doing less business with the companies that were not able to support our goal of 100% recycled or bio-based raw materials'.

Customer demand provides a business opportunity too. Major retailers like Marks & Spencer are increasingly positioning themselves as 'gate-keepers' for consumers, removing the need for the general public to understand the sustainability impact of the products they buy. De-risking supply chains can be a business opportunity for business-to-business (B2B) businesses too.

Moral imperative

Throughout history, there have always been companies with a strong sense of moral purpose. Famous examples include Henry Ford's desire to democratise transport, or Cadbury's desire to provide working people with drinking chocolate as an alternative to alcohol. Modern equivalents such as Body Shop and Whole Food Markets see a moral imperative in enhancing society and the environment. These organisations say they do not exist to make profit, but rather they make profit in order to carry out their higher purpose.

The moral imperative viewpoint often makes decision-making more straightforward. 'Because everything we do is underpinned by Kyocera's philosophy of harmonious co-existence, we don't have to think up new systems and processes', says Tracy Rawling Church of document management systems provider KyoceraDUK. '"The right thing to do" is quite a simple concept – and it's very liberating.'

All of us, from individual consumers to colossal multinational corporations have buying power. Why not use that buying power for good? For example, on a recent business trip to Stockholm, I noticed the preponderance of 'green taxis'. When I asked my host how this had come about, he told me that so many companies have a policy of hiring only green taxis that it makes little sense for taxi companies to buy conventional cars. Thus green becomes the norm.

In the same way, if you help build supply chains for sustainable products and services that render conventional equivalents redundant, then you are helping shape the entire economy. For example, Marks & Spencer talk about 'racing to scale' their contribution to a circular economy (more on this in Chapter 2). If M&S's demand for, say, high grade recovered polyester fibre helps bring the price below that of virgin material, then recycling will become the norm, not the exception.

The bottom line

Sustainability risks in the supply chain usually exceed those within the factory fence. It is therefore imperative from a business and ethical point of view to address the sustainability of your supply chain in a rigorous way.

As we covered at the start of the chapter, the business case varies from company to company. You need a clear understanding of the most important drivers for your organisation as this shapes your vision, strategy and action plans. For example, if your foremost concern is the security of supply of a key material, it will require quite different actions than if your highest priority is to protect your brand from poor emissions control in suppliers.

It is also worth noting that the business case does not stand still. The relative importance of different drivers may change over time due to technology, demand, public perception, etc. However, the overall direction will be for higher standards – driven by tighter legislation, costs and higher stakeholder expectations – businesses need to keep raising the bar. And if you don't do it, someone else will.

CHAPTER 2

Supply Chains and Sustainability

Where the problem lies

FOR MOST ORGANISATIONS, the majority of their environmental impact is in their supply chain rather than within the factory fence/office walls. For example, carbon footprinting used to focus on on-site carbon emissions (commonly known as Scope 1) and those associated with electricity use on site (Scope 2). However, as Figure 3 demonstrates, supply chain emissions (Scope 3) tend to outstrip the others in significance and cannot be ignored.

FIGURE 3. Carbon footprints of four major organisations.[12]

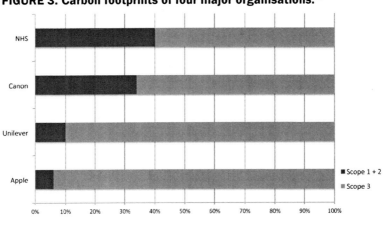

The most damaging industries tend to be in the primary sector: agriculture, forestry, fishing, mining and the extraction of oil and gas, along with the initial processing of the products concerned. For example, the mining of ores requires all the 'overburden' of soil and rock to be removed first – this is usually several times as much material as the ore deposit itself. Extracting useable materials from that ore is also difficult and dirty. The production of 1 kg of pure copper from its ore results in 50–200 kg of waste and requires 50–100 MJ of energy, which in turn will release about 13 kg of carbon dioxide into the atmosphere.[13]

This presents a real challenge for companies further up the value chain trying to green the supply chain. As Tom Smith of Sedex puts it, 'As you go down the supply chain, the sustainability risks are greater, you have less visibility, and you have less influence.'

Key environmental issues

There is a wide range of environmental issues that you need to consider. The following list is a very simple guide to the key issues.

Climate change

The biggest and most intractable problem we face is arguably climate change. The science behind climate change – that the accumulation of man-made greenhouse gases is leading to more heat trapped in the atmosphere – is well established. Unfortunately, in the political and media spheres there is a visceral debate on that science and its implications, which seeds doubt in the mind of the public.

The political target for limiting climate change is a rise of 2°C above preindustrial average temperatures. The current trajectory is for a temperature rise of 2.5–4.7°C by 2100.[14] To have a reasonable chance of meeting the political targets, carbon emissions would need to peak by 2020 and then reduce to 50% of 1990 levels by 2050.[15]

Resource use

We have seen in Chapter 1 that our use of resources is unsustainable from an economic point of view. Clearly there are environmental implications as well as economic impacts. As resources become scarcer, we go look for them in more risky locations, for example, the deep-sea oil drilling that led to the 2010 Deepwater Horizon disaster in the Gulf of Mexico. Over-exploiting biological resources can have a devastating impact on eco-systems, for example, felling rainforest or overfishing, as vital components are removed, upsetting natural balances.

Regional impacts on certain resources can be severe too, for example, irrigation and industry often compete for water in arid areas, leaving even less for natural eco-systems and for drinking water for local populations.

While we might think we are far from a dystopian Mad Max-style societal breakdown, it has been estimated that about 20 wars have been fuelled by resource scarcity in the last 50 years.[16]

Persistent bioaccumulative toxic (PBT) compounds

As the name suggests, these chemicals do not break down easily in the environment, but build up in the food chain, poisoning organisms as they go. The most famous PBT substance is DDT, the main subject of Rachel Carson's seminal book *Silent Spring*,[17] which launched the modern environmental movement. Other PBTs include many pesticides, flame-retardants and products of incineration such as dioxins. These materials are also surprisingly mobile, migrating towards the polar regions where they contaminate an environment that has never had significant direct exposure.

Land use changes

Feeding a rising population and providing them with products such as paper, palm oil and cotton has led to massive land use changes from indigenous forest or grassland to 'green concrete' intensive agriculture. This has a number of impacts: loss of natural habitats, damage to soil structure, loss of carbon from soils, aesthetic impacts, erosion, and a wide range of 'eco-system services'. For example, it has been estimated that half of the world's tropical forests have been lost in the industrial era.[18] A key issue is 'indirect land use changes' or ILUC – this is when one land use change, for example, using agricultural land to produce biofuels, leads to another, for example, if the displaced food production leads to deforestation in our example. This is an important issue, but one that is very difficult to quantify and control.

Biodiversity loss

We are currently in the sixth mass extinction period on Earth. This one has been attributed to the evolution of man and is thought to be much worse than the previous five. The current rate of loss of species is thought to be about 1000 times the background rate[19] – some say more. The causes of this are manifold: loss of habitat, over-exploitation and climate change – in many ways, biodiversity loss is a symptom of the other environmental issues.

Ozone depletion

Just a couple of decades ago, ozone depletion was high on the environ-mental agenda. Man-made chemicals, predominantly chlorofluorocarbons (CFCs), were reacting with the protective layer of ozone that screens out harmful UV rays from the sun. The Montreal Protocol of 1987 led to a reduction in the production of CFCs and a stabilisation of the 'ozone hole' of Antarctica[20] but concerns remain about the thinning of ozone in the Northern Hemisphere.[21]

Local/regional pollution

As well as global problems such as climate change or ozone depletion, there is a wide range of local or regional pollution risks. Some important issues are:

- Acid rain from sulphur emissions can have a devastating effect on regional eco-systems.

- The contamination of rivers, lakes and groundwater will have environmental and economic impacts.

- Urban air quality is a problem that predominantly affects people's health.

Geographically limited impacts are complicated by the sensitivity of the locality to the problem. For example, polluting an aquifer in the South of England that relies on already overstretched groundwater supplies will have a more severe impact than the same incident in areas with a plentiful supply of surface water.

Models of a sustainable economy

In Chapter 1 we discussed how the ultimate aim of addressing environmental issues in the supply chain should be to contribute to an environmentally sustainable economy. So, if this were successful, what would the big picture look like?

There are two main models for a sustainable economy:

- Eco-efficiency – an economy which extracts much greater value from each unit of resource until resource consumption falls to a sustainable level.

- Eco-systems model – an economy that emulates the cycles of nature.

We will look at each of these in turn.

Eco-efficiency

Eco-efficiency is defined as the amount of use you can get from a unit of resource. Miles per gallon (mpg) is probably the most well known example of eco-efficiency as it represents the distance you can travel (use) on one unit of fuel (resource). So if you switch to a more efficient car and you don't change your driving habits, you will use less fuel.

It is also the most popular model, if by default, probably because it is relatively easy to measure. However, the eco-efficiency model is undermined by the 'rebound effect' in which efficiency gains lead to resources being used faster by encouraging our use of the technology, rather than using fewer resources as intended. For example, a modern family car is four times more efficient than a Ford Model T, yet emissions from car use have gone up by about a factor of five since the heyday of the Model T.[22]

Eco-systems models

Nature is not very efficient. Think of the number of acorns an oak tree produces compared to the number of mature trees that result from all those seeds. And yet nature is sustainable – it has been relatively stable for a couple of billion years.

The basis of nature's sustainability is materials flowing in continuous loops – the carbon cycle, the water cycle, the nitrogen cycle, etc. These are powered by renewable sources of energy, predominately heat from the sun. Toxins do not accumulate and diversity gives the system robustness – if one element of the eco-system fails, there is often another which can take on the same role.

Translating this into an industrial economy, the loops are replicated by the 'circular economy' where every material used is recovered or returned to nature in a useful form (e.g. as compost). The only energy source is renewable energy and persistent toxic substances are designed out.

Choice of model

There is no need to make a hard and fast choice between the two models – you can use fewer resources and emulate nature at the same time. Many opportunities will deliver against both: for example, recycling metals contributes to the circular economy and will also use less energy than producing raw materials from ore.

The default position for sustainability has tended to be the eco-efficiency model as it lends itself to quantitative monitoring. However, the leaders in the sustainability business world are increasingly favouring the eco-system model approach, as it will deliver sustainability without rebound effects. This can be seen through the large-scale push towards a 'circular economy' and the rapid uptake of renewable energy.

CHAPTER 3

Building a Sustainable Supply Chain

Overview

IN THIS CHAPTER we will look at the fundamentals underpinning the practical actions to build a sustainable supply chain, before we move on to practical measures in the following chapters. We will look at setting the scope of the process, basic principles, management systems and metrics, employee engagement and training.

Different organisations have different procurement processes. Some may have pre-qualification stages followed by a formal request for tender and tender evaluation; others will be much more informal. In this book we make no assumptions about the procurement process itself; however, a general rule of thumb is the earlier in the cycle environmental issues are considered, the better.

Scope – What's in and what's out

One of the key issues in greening the supply chain is deciding what should be included in the programme and what can be left out. Tracing the provenance of every last paperclip in every far-flung regional office operated by every third-tier supplier is both pointless and impractical.

If you want to make a real difference to your supply chain you need to apply some 80:20 thinking, in other words focus on the relatively small number of issues that have the biggest impact as it is here that you will make the biggest improvements. For example, a tissue paper manufacturer should include the provenance of the pulp it uses (forestry or recycled paper), but it shouldn't waste much time on, say, whether a minor supplier uses paper or plastic coffee cups in its cafeteria. The importance of an issue is often referred to as 'significance' or 'materiality'.

While the narrowing of focus is a necessity, it is also a risk. If you do it in completely subjective way, you risk missing a crucial issue and it either blowing up in your face or being accused of greenwash – or both. There are a number of ways of determining this scope in a more objective manner:

- Carry out a lifecycle assessment/carbon footprint of your product or service to determine where the most significant issues arise in the chain that runs from materials extraction through manufacturing, use and to eventual disposal.

- Use a screening indicator, for example, procurement spend, to filter out 'the small stuff'.

- Carry out a risk assessment to determine where the greatest potential commercial damage lies against the drivers assessed in Chapter 1.

- Survey your stakeholders to ensure all issues they have concerns about are covered.

- If you follow a sustainability reporting standard such as the Global Reporting Initiative G4 protocol,[23] it will have guidance on how to choose which issues are 'material'.

- Use a supply chain management service such as Sedex. These allow members to carry out a risk assessment on suppliers' data to identify 'hot spots' for a 'deep dive' analysis (see box in Chapter 4).

Basic supply chain principles

Our discussion of a sustainable economy in the last chapter concluded that you have two basic options to green your supply chain: eco-efficiency and emulating eco-systems.

The following tactics will make your supply chain more eco-efficient:

- Purchase less stuff (per unit output).

- Purchase stuff that causes less damage to produce.

- Purchase stuff that will require less energy in use (either in your processes or as part of your product).

The eco-system model approach requires that you aim to do *all* of the below:

- Purchase natural, biodegradable stuff from sustainable sources and/or purchase recycled/secondary materials.

- Purchase zero carbon energy, and/or devices which use zero carbon energy.

- Phase out all toxic materials.

These simple principles are complicated by a number of internal and external barriers which we will describe below.

Constraints on building a sustainable supply chain

Internal constraints

FIGURE 4. Internal constraints on a buying decision.

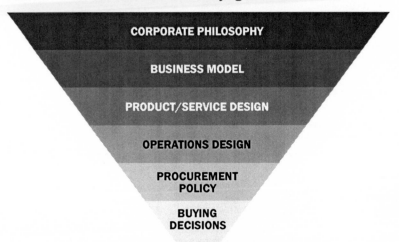

Why does your organisation buy products and services from others? Fundamentally, it is to enable you to deliver your product and/or service to your customers. Therefore the procurement process is constrained by what the rest of the organisation demands. Figure 4 shows the hierarchy of constraints – the more radical you wish to be, the higher you need to effect change in the hierarchy. From bottom to top, the levels are:

- Showing preference for more sustainable products and services during purchasing decisions is the easiest place to start, but it will only ever lead to incremental improvements.

- By setting a procurement policy which, say excludes certain substances or certain suppliers, you will have more influence, but you are still constrained by the way the rest of the organisation operates.

- Your operations – whether manufacturing, logistics or even office processes – will determine which materials you need and in what quantities.

- Above that, the actual design of your product and/or service will drive operations and the levels below. Will this product be designed to be made out of recycled materials? Does it require rare earth metals?

- The business model is the next influential factor – are you going to produce a physical product at all or a digital product or a product service system where you lease rather than sell?

- And overarching everything else is your corporate philosophy – are you prepared to invest in the supply chain you need? Do you want to be a pioneer of the circular economy? Or collaborative consumption? Are you going to use your buying power to effect change on a transformational level?

Of course in practice, the boundaries blur and they may not all apply to all organisations. But the overall principle is that the higher in the hierarchy you effect change, the bigger the impact on your supply chain footprint. In the following chapters we will be considering change at these different levels, taking them in pairs.

External constraints

The following external risks apply to attempts to green the supply chain:

- Traceability: in long and complex supply chains, it can be very difficult to trace exactly where materials originate. 'Our dirty secret is that we often don't know who our suppliers are' is the honest admission of Gavin Neath, vice president of sustainability at Unilever.[24]

- Cultural differences: attitudes to different environmental pressures and environmental legislation vary from country to country. 'Some countries are very strict on compliance', says Sean Axon of Johnson Matthey. 'Others are more interpretive of rules and guidelines.'

- Translating information between languages can also introduce uncertainty. 'Numbers are numbers in any language', says KyoceraDUK's Tracy Rawling Church, 'but when it comes to qualitative measures, it gets more difficult.'

- Immaturity: the supply chains for many 'greener' materials are immature leading to lack of competition/choice, high prices, low quality and scarcity of supply.

- Dominance of existing suppliers: many suppliers have huge economic strength which reduces the power of their (often smaller) customers to force or persuade them to change.

- Legislation can hinder greener opportunities. For example in the UK, once a material is designated 'waste' it requires a waste licence to handle it until either it becomes a new product or when it meets one of a growing number of quality standards.

Sustainable supply chain management

Sustainable procurement will require management procedures to make sure it happens. The sections below cover the main elements required.

Procurement policy

It is essential to set down a written policy on sustainable procurement and make it publicly available. A robust, clear policy means that potential suppliers will have a clear idea of what you expect from them before they even think about applying/bidding to do business with you. It also sends a clear message to internal stakeholders that the organisation is serious about reducing its impact on the supply chain.

A sustainable procurement policy will typically have the following sections:

- A high level statement of what the policy is intended to achieve.

- Broad principles of intent and/or high level targets.

- Minimum standards required of all suppliers, for example, have an environmental policy, hold an environmental management system certificate (although a threshold may be required to avoid prejudicing small businesses).

- Individual product group targets derived from corporate targets (see below), for example, for food, paper, transport services, etc. These targets may stipulate eco-product standards (see Chapter 4).

- How the policy will be implemented during procurement exercises.

- An endorsement by senior management, preferably the Chief Executive.

Management systems

In 2010 the British Standards Institute published BS 8903: Principles and Framework for Procuring Sustainably.[25] This standard defines sustainable procurement as 'only purchasing goods that are needed, and buying items or services whose production, use and disposal both minimise negative impacts and encourage positive outcomes for the environment, economy and society'. It has four main aims:

- To minimise the demand for resources.

- To minimise negative impacts.

- To respect ethical standards.

- To promote diversity and equality.

As with all such management systems, the standard requires a set of written targets and procedures for each aspect of sustainable procurement and for the holder to audit performance against those standards. Unlike, say, ISO 14001, the standard is for guidance only and there is no certification system.

Whether or not you choose to follow a formal standard such as BS 8903, some form of management system will be required to ensure that sustainable procurement is embedded into the decision-making process. The standard underlying format is Deming's Plan, Do, Check, Act cycle. The stages are as follows:

- Plan: establish the objectives, targets and procedures necessary to deliver results in accordance with those targets.

- Do: implement the plan, gathering the data required to assess the success against targets.

- Check: compare actual results against targets and trace problems back to root causes.

- Act (sometimes 'Adjust'): make corrective actions to fix any discrepancies.

The idea of the cycle is to tighten the targets at each iteration to deliver continual improvement.

Targets and metrics

Whether you follow a standard like BS 8903 or the Global Reporting Initiative G4, or develop your own system, it is essential to set targets and measure progress against those targets. You will require two types of metric:

- Environmental impact metrics.

- Management metrics.

Obviously the environmental impact targets must be representative of the issues identified in the scoping/materiality exercise and should be aligned with your main corporate sustainability targets. Examples include:

- % wood products purchased that meet a recognised standard such as FSC.

- % reduction in the carbon footprint of the supply chain.

Management metrics measure progress in implementing your green procurement strategy. Examples include:

- % of procurement spend with sustainability targets embedded.

- % of suppliers audited/assessed.

- % of buyers trained in sustainable purchasing.

To deliver effective change in the supply chain, the environmental impact targets should be given higher priority than the management targets. After all, you will ultimately be judged on external changes, not on how many boxes have been ticked.

Both types of targets should be made the responsibility of procurement managers (or operations/product managers where appropriate) rather than being the responsibility of the CSR function. This will embed accountability in the place where it needs to be – the procurement teams.

Another issue is whether to make incremental change or step changes. While the former may appear less risky, it can inhibit progress on cost grounds. Stretch targets often lead to better solutions. For example, when Gregg's responded to a request for fair trade products such as tea, coffee, hot chocolate and sugar, the company implemented this across all their outlets. 'It only made sense to do it across the business,' said Gregg's Stephen Weldon, 'rather than just for a single shop.'

Enabling change

Employee engagement

I often say that the biggest barrier to sustainability is just 6 inches wide – the space between our ears. You can have the best possible green procurement system, but it will be useless if employee behaviour doesn't change accordingly to implement it effectively.

I call my approach to employee engagement and behavioural change

'Green Jujitsu' and I have written a Dō Short on the topic.[26] The basic principle of Green Jujitsu is that you work with the prevailing culture of the organisation and to the strengths and interests of your colleagues; much in the way a jujitsu practitioner sees their opponent's strength, height and weight as an opportunity not a threat.

The following Green Jujitsu techniques can be applied to greening the supply chain:

- Match the tone of your communications to the tone of your business culture (e.g. an engineering company should take a technical approach featuring data and bar charts, whereas a high street fashion company may respond better to, say, stylish infographics).

- Provide feedback to all employees so they can see how the sustainability programme is progressing. This feedback should be in a format that appeals to the audience (as above).

- Use storytelling to show how colleagues have made improvements in particular supply chain areas from the perspective of that employee. Hearing about 'people like us' achieving something is a powerful message.

- Make it easier to follow the green procurement processes than to sidestep them. Eliminate any unnecessary bureaucracy and make the process obligatory (e.g. in IT systems).

- Use practical workshops to both engage colleagues and generate potential solutions to problems. For the techniques described in Chapters 5 and 6, this provides an opportunity to bring colleagues from across the business together to unlock progress in particular areas.

- Tap into existing team loyalties by, for example, running competitions between different procurement teams.

Training

Clearly all staff involved in procurement will need to be trained in the new systems and broader environmental issues in the supply chain. To make training effective I recommend the following:

- Make all case studies, examples and exercises directly relevant to supply chain sustainability in the sector concerned.

- Make the session highly interactive – for example, by getting teams to plot out the supply chains that they manage. The ratio of exercises to presentations should be greater than 1:1.

- Blur the boundaries between training and the solutions workshops described above.

- Avoid the guilt trip. Sustainability should be portrayed as 'more stilettos than sandals', as Ashley Lodge of HarperCollins put it.

....

CHAPTER 4

Basic Techniques:
Procurement and Buying

Overview

THIS CHAPTER COVERS the practical actions required to implement green procurement principles within the procurement function itself. These are often described as the 'hard yards' of sustainable supply chain management as much of the work is unglamorous, but needs to be done to get the basics right.

Through-life costing

Many organisations focus on driving down purchase costs and neglect the full cost of using, maintaining and disposing of the item. For example, a particular vehicle may be chosen on purchase price alone, but end up costing the business more due to its fuel consumption. Unfortunately procurement officers are often financially incentivised to secure discount on purchase costs.

By shifting to procurement based on through-life costs, the organisation will tend to buy equipment which is more efficient in use, leading to reduced energy consumption, reduced purchases of consumables and reduced waste. Procurement teams should be incentivised to minimise the total cost of ownership, not just purchase costs.

Black and grey lists

The car manufacturer Volvo pioneered the use of 'grey' and 'black' lists to filter out materials and chemicals that are not safe.[27] Black list substances should never be purchased and those on the grey list should only be used where no alternative exists. Anybody who wants a grey list substance should be required to provide a written justification for doing so. Some organisations help purchasers (and product designers) by providing a 'green list' or 'white list' of preferred substances.

Black and grey lists are highly industry specific, so you will need to research toxic materials in your business and determine which can and can't be replaced. Some sectoral bodies produce these lists, for example, the Oslo and Paris Commission (OSPAR) publishes black, grey and green lists for oil/gas drilling fluids.[28]

Use of product eco-labels

A popular method of ensuring basic levels of supply chain sustainability is to insist on products meeting relevant third-party standards, such as:

- Forest Stewardship Council (FSC) standard for wood products including paper.

- Energy Star for IT equipment.

- Soil Association standard for organic food.

- EU Energy Label for a range of products from white goods to public buildings.

- EU Eco-label for products ranging from televisions to shampoos.

- Marine Stewardship Council (MSC) standard for seafood.

There are a number of advantages of this approach:

- An independent third party has set the standard in an objective way, reducing the risk of 'greenwash'.

- It is up to the supplier to prove to the accreditation body that they have made the grade.

- Product standards work up and down the supply chain.

However, it is important to remember that such standards are almost inevitably unambitious. In fact, a sustainability manager from a major chemical manufacturer recently told me that his company actively lobbies to keep new standards as low as possible. If you really want to build a sustainable supply chain you need to be driving performance higher, but often it makes sense to use such standards as a basic minimum. So while insisting on an eco-label is a good starting point, it should not be seen as an end in itself.

Assessing and ranking suppliers

The most common approach to assessing suppliers is to ask them to complete a questionnaire. Typical assessment questions are:[29]

- Does your company have an environmental policy? If yes, please attach a copy.

- Does your company have environmental targets? If yes, please provide details.

- Do you review/audit your environmental performance? If yes, please provide details.

- Has your company attained any environmental management standard(s) (e.g. ISO 14001/EMAS)? If yes, please attach details.

- Has your company had any convictions in the last three years for non-compliance with environmental legislation? If yes, please provide details.

- Please identify the significant adverse environmental impacts associated with the delivery of this contract?

- How will you minimise, mitigate and manage these significant adverse environmental impacts?

This approach however puts quite a strain on suppliers who often receive a steady stream of such questionnaires, each requiring different sets of data in different formats. Ideally, you'd like your suppliers to be working on improving their performance rather than filling in questionnaires. A number of third-party services have sprung up to address this problem by providing a database of supplier responses to standard questions, for example, Sedex (see box).

Of course, you have to trust that the data received in questionnaires is reliable. Some organisations reduce this risk by auditing key suppliers' sites, either using internal employees or a third-party auditor. For example, after those fierce criticisms of the environmental performance and labour practices of its Chinese suppliers, Apple has ramped up supplier audits by a factor of 10 since 2007 and publishes the results online.[30] Services such as Sedex allow suppliers to upload third-party audit reports to avoid duplication.

To translate the results of supplier assessments into a form of guidance for procurement staff, many companies have adopted a formal ranking system. For example, Sharp ranks its suppliers from A to D; A rated suppliers are designated 'Green Suppliers' and are given preference, those rated B and C are expected to improve, and the default position is not to purchase from a supplier ranked D.[31]

CASE STUDY: Sedex

Sedex is a not-for-profit service which helps its members manage environmental and ethical issues in its supply chain. It was established by a group of major UK retailers who wanted to simplify the ethical/environmental auditing of their suppliers and eliminate duplication. It now has about 29,000 members in 156 countries. 580 of these members are big brands or retailers and the rest are suppliers.

Sedex's core product is a secure online database that allows members to store, share and report on information on four key areas:

- Labour standards
- Health & safety
- The environment
- Business ethics

Suppliers complete standard audit questionnaires and upload supporting information such as certificates and audit reports. The supplier can then release the data to customers and potential customers on request.

Tom Smith, Head of Marketing and Business Development at Sedex, says:

It is all about data, really. If you are a small company and have three or four main suppliers then you can speak to people, meet them and you know what's going on. But if you're a large business and you have thousands or hundreds of thousands of suppliers and you're asking everyone to get audited and you're getting ten issues per audit, then there's a huge amount of data to keep track of. We can mine that data for hotspots and then our clients can deep-dive into those key issues.

Blacklisting suppliers

Some suppliers are so toxic that they must be proactively identified and ruled out of contention. For example, in recent years Asian Pulp & Paper (APP), the world's third largest paper manufacturer, was blacklisted by a huge number of top brands, everybody from Fuji to Gucci via Volkswagen. Those brands didn't want to be associated with APP's destructive clear felling of rainforest. In 2012 APP declared an immediate halt to clearing natural forests in South East Asia, demonstrating that the boycott had had a positive impact.[32]

If you are serious about greening the supply chain, you need to have the ultimate sanction of blacklisting suppliers – and communicate it to current and potential future suppliers. While some suppliers can be blacklisted for failing to meet minimum standards, that is, those Sharp would rank as 'D', others, as in the case above, are so potentially damaging to a company's reputation that they need to identified proactively.

Creating an 'arms race'

Most of the techniques here depend on the purchaser to specify the environmental performance of a product or service. But how do you drive your suppliers to go further and faster on their own volition?

Public sector organisations usually implement a formal scoring system for tenders. The available points are typically split between different criteria such as cost, performance, track record, and risk. A number of such bodies have started allocating 10%, 15% or even 30% of the total score to green and/or ethical issues – above and beyond minimum standards. This means that a bidder can win the contract by beating the opposition on green alone, creating an 'arms race' between suppliers over time as each tries to up their game to stay competitive. For example, Glen Bennett of EAE Ltd says that when he's tendering to Scottish public sector bodies, he finds a picture of the company's wind turbine is worth 100 environmental policies.

The assessment can either be against the supplier's performance overall, or it can be applied to the specific product, for example for a vehicle:

We require the vehicle to have carbon emissions of no more than 150 gCO$_2$/km. For every 10 g below this target we will award an extra 10 points.[33]

Transparency and traceability

A few years ago I had a meeting with the environmental manager of a major contract tissue paper manufacturer. 'You give me the code on the packaging on any one of our products,' he told me, 'and I'll tell you the hectare of forest that the wood pulp came from.' This rigorous supply chain transparency is part of the service they offer their customers, neatly turning a potential risk into a business opportunity.

As we saw in Chapter 3, many businesses struggle to achieve transparency and traceability in their supply chains. A basic technique is to include transparency questions in supplier questionnaires, and traceability clauses in contract conditions. The exact requirement will vary from material to material.

If you purchase particularly sensitive materials, for example, tropical hardwoods, palm oil or minerals that are sometimes sourced from war zones (conflict minerals), it is worth carrying out 'Chain of Custody' reviews to trace the material right back to its source. The result of the review is a paper trail documenting the movements and ownership of the material from when it was first harvested/extracted until it becomes your property. This will help ensure that dubiously sourced materials are not getting into your supply chain without you knowing it.

The need for traceability may require difficult decisions to make data manageable. 'We want 100% traceability', says Gail Klintworth, Unilever's global chief sustainability officer. To this end the company is reducing the number of palm oil suppliers by 80%, a rather brutal move, but necessary as the company sees it.[34]

Smarter purchasing

Buying material simply to throw it away is bad business and has an associated environmental impact. For example, it has been estimated that the construction industry throws away one eighth of all materials it purchases without them ever being used.[35] Simply sharpening up your act can bring instant improvements:

- Checking you really do need the product (you'd be surprised how much stuff gets bought and never used).

- Ensuring dimensions and quantities match your needs.

- Carefully managing stocks of perishable items so they don't exceed their shelf life.

- Facilitating the reuse of resources within the organisation or between organisations (see WARPit case study below).

- Keeping stocks as low as possible to avoid damage in stores or supplies becoming redundant due to changes elsewhere in the organisation.

For example, I have worked with several companies who I found were purchasing components too long for their needs and cutting them to length every time. Simply by specifying the correct length of component, less material was being bought in the first place, the cutting was eliminated and less waste was produced, saving time, money and resources.

A powerful tool to use during such investigations is the 'Toddler Test' aka 'The 5 Whys' – keep asking 'Why' until you get to the core reason – which is quite often easily fixed, for example:

- Why do we cut all these components? Because they are too long.

- Why are they too long? Because we buy them at that length.

- Why do we buy them at that length? Dunno – because we always have.

CASE STUDY: WARPit

WARPit (**www.warp-it.co.uk**) was launched in 2011 to provide a platform for the reuse of items such as office furniture. Instead of disposing of serviceable but unwanted items, subscribers can load details onto the system for other members to peruse – either within their own organisation or between organisations. Founder Dan O'Connor describes WARPit as 'a kind of hybrid of eBay, Freecycle and Facebook for organisations'.

'The main benefit of WARPit is that organisations do not have to buy what they, or partners in the network, already have spare – reducing procurement and waste costs', says O'Connor. 'Customers are making great financial savings, up to £10,000 per month in some cases. Environmentally, to take an example, the amount of waste generated to produce a single laptop computer is close to 4000 times its weight. This is why it is important to redistribute "stuff"' in this way.'

In the first two years of operation WARPit has saved customers over £0.5 million in procurement costs, 250 tonnes of CO_2 and 100 tonnes of waste.

Outcomes based procurement

Organisations often put artificial constraints on their suppliers, for example, by specifying 'we require 100 photocopier/printers capable of x pages per minute'. This specification is usually based on the status quo and can restrict suppliers in delivering the most sustainable solution. There are substantial potential benefits in moving to 'outcomes based procurement' where the specification may be 'we require a document copying/printing system for 1000 employees' and letting the suppliers work out what the best solution is.

For example, when procuring a new lighting system, instead of specifying how many lamps of a particular wattage it required, Rotherham NHS Trust specified the following outcomes:[36]

- A step change in patient experience: creating a pleasant healing environment with patients being in control of bed zone lighting levels and ambience and providing the lighting to perform clinical requirements and incorporating measures to reduce the risk of hospital acquired infections.

- A demonstrable step change in energy efficiency with progressive improvements in energy efficiency and operational performance over the life of the project.

- A fully installed and future-ready solution.

It was up to those tendering for the contract to decide how best these outcomes could be delivered and justify it in their proposal. Early signs are that it will result in substantial energy savings.

Forward commitment procurement

Tackling sustainability in the supply chain often stumbles against the paradox that until there is demand for more sustainable alternatives, there will be no supply, but without supply, procurement teams will simply follow business as usual so there is no demand for change. A useful tool to help break this paradox is 'forward commitment procurement' –

announcing to suppliers in advance what the organisation would like out of a future product/service, how much it would want and by when. This de-risks the development of new product/services for suppliers, as they know there will be a market for that product/service if they get it right.

For example, HM Prison Service used to buy 60,000 polyurethane foam mattresses and pillows per year and disposed of around 40,000, mainly to landfill, but a significant number had to be disposed of as clinical waste. This was wasteful from both an environmental and an economic point of view, costing about £3 million per year. So in 2006, the Service set out the following requirement:

> *HMPS aspires to a zero waste prison mattress that meets or exceeds current operational requirements and delivers whole life cycle cost efficiencies. By 2012, HMPS wants all its mattresses and pillows not classified as hazardous waste to be recycled, repurposed or reused instead of going to landfill; and to reduce to 2 per cent pa the number of mattresses disposed of as hazardous or clinical waste.*

The contract with the winning supplier was signed in 2009 and has been estimated to save HMPS £5 million over its duration. Success against the environmental requirements is still being assessed as the contract progresses.[37]

Note that to be effective, an outcomes based specification (see above) is a prerequisite of forward commitment procurement.

....

CHAPTER 5

Intermediate Techniques: Operations and Product/Service

Overview

AS WE SAW IN CHAPTER 3, the decision of what and how much to purchase is constrained by the demands of the organisation's operations that are in turn constrained by the product/service delivered. In this chapter we will look at how changes at this operations and product/service level will enable a more sustainable supply chain. The techniques presented here require the involvement of people outside the procurement team. They also tend to be more risky than the approaches we have seen previously.

Operations management

As we have discussed above, the purpose of procurement is to enable the organisation's functions to take place. Changes at this level will have more effect on the company's supply chain than the procurement process itself. Obviously opportunities are highly dependent on the sector concerned but here are some examples:

- Running waste minimisation programmes to track back to source and tackling the underlying problem will cut the amount of raw material being purchased.

- Replacing resources with data, for example, implementing better control systems to reduce off-spec product.

- Changing to a cleaner process technology, for example, using 'green chemistry' or biotechnology to produce chemical products.

- Designing manufacturing processes to accept a wider range of tolerances on raw material quality to open up the possibility of more sustainable sources of material, for example, recycled polyester.

Industrial symbiosis

Industrial symbiosis is the idea of copying the fundamental principle in natural eco-systems that the 'waste' from one organism always becomes 'food' for another organism. A field of cattle can produce 100 tonnes of manure per year, yet that 'waste' does not accumulate. Instead a variety of organisms treat that manure as a food source, breaking it down into substances, which feed the grass, which in turn feeds the cows.

It is impossible to discuss industrial symbiosis without mentioning Kalundborg, Denmark, as it was here that industrial symbiosis was first uncovered as a phenomenon. The heavy industries near the town were incentivised to relocate there by the government in the 1970s to tackle unemployment, but there was one big problem: a lack of fresh water. The industries tackled this problem by collaborating to cascade water from one process to another, starting where it had to be cleanest and working its way down through the less sensitive processes, recycling it wherever possible.

This initial collaboration catalysed a web of other material and energy flows between businesses, which you can see in Figure 5. A huge district heating system distributes steam from the power station to the other plants, some agricultural greenhouses and to the town where it heats all the buildings. The fish farm uses (and cools) some of the warm wastewater. A plasterboard company takes the gypsum from the power station's pollution control system in place of virgin gypsum. A pharmaceutical plant produces a fertiliser product made from its process substrate. This is produced to strict product standards, trademarked, but given away free to local farmers. If the company had to pay for disposal, it would go bust.

FIGURE 5. Simplified diagram of industrial symbiosis at Kalundborg.[38]

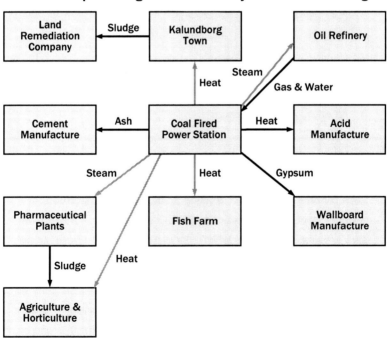

This turns the whole idea of a supply chain on its head. Instead of a simple linear flow of materials from extraction through manufacturing use and to disposal, industrial symbiosis creates a tangled web of material and energy flows where 'waste' and 'raw materials' become synonymous.

To implement industrial symbiosis, you will need the following:

- A good understanding of your process requirements, in particular raw material tolerances.

- A preparedness to pre-process materials if necessary to bring them within tolerances.

- A network of local contacts, or a broker service to identify opportunities.

- A good relationship with regulators as they need to accept the 'disposal route' as they see it as legitimate.

- An open, inventive mind.

CASE STUDY: National Industrial Symbiosis Programme

The UK's National Industrial Symbiosis Programme (NISP) has been running since 2005, making it the first IS programme on a national level. In that time over 15,000 organisations have taken part, leading to synergies which represent a diversion from landfill of 9 million tonnes per annum, saving 12 million tonnes of raw material per annum and 8 million tonnes of CO_2 per annum.

'Our strapline "connecting industry to create opportunity" sums NISP up', says founder Peter Laybourn. 'Those opportunities can be

---

in innovation, new business opportunities and/or cost reduction.'

The projects NISP has facilitated include 300,000 tomato plants being grown under glass using waste heat and carbon dioxide from a local fertiliser plant, the recovery of silver and rare earth metals from a range of sources such as hearing aid batteries, and an animal renderer which has become a net energy producer.

Initially funded by the UK government, the programme now operates on a subscription basis. NISP's parent company, International Synergies Ltd, has now launched similar industrial symbiosis programmes in 15 different countries across five continents.

Product takeback

Flooring company InterfaceFLOR's ambitious Mission Zero commitment requires that 100% of raw materials are natural and/or recycled. When the company analysed the options available, it concluded that the best sustainable source was old carpet. The company developed the ReEntry 2.0 takeback system, which is now reprocessing almost 500 tonnes of carpet per week. Once the material is recovered, the face and the backing of the carpet are separated and recycled back into carpet components.

Taking back and reprocessing products in this way is a clear step towards a circular economy. However, the following factors are a pre-requisite:

- Materials are recyclable.

- Products are easily dismantled.

- Good waste segregation at the product's end-of-life location.

- The 'reverse logistics' of recovering the product are economically viable.

The first two factors can be improved by designing the product to be recovered – we will be looking at product design later in this chapter. The third and fourth factor is dependent on quite a few external factors, including customer behaviour, government legislation, fuel prices and the nature of the product. For example, a number of plasterboard takeback schemes have sprung up as legislation drives waste segregation and recycling on building sites.[39]

Engaging your existing supply chain

There are often opportunities to work with suppliers to find win-win solutions. A classic example is that Walker's Crisps were buying potatoes at gross weight so their suppliers were keeping the potatoes hydrated to maximise value. That water needed to be driven off during frying, requiring extra energy. Walker's talked to their suppliers and agreed to buy potatoes by dry weight instead. As a result the hydration stopped, saving energy and water, and the frying took less energy too.[40]

Similarly, Greggs had a supplier of salad ingredients who used cardboard trays as packaging, but these were causing a waste-handling problem in its bakeries. Greggs and the supplier negotiated to switch to plastic trays similar to those that the company already uses to handle their own products. These could be cleaned and sanitised by existing equipment and returned to the supplier.

The sustainability ambitions of InterfaceFLOR inspired one of their suppliers, Aquafil, to start making yarn from old fishing nets pulled from the ocean. 'We continue to be impressed by what can be achieved when suppliers are encouraged to innovate and are rewarded for solving *our* problems instead of us trying to solve theirs. We have witnessed how much more the "inspire, measure, innovate" approach can deliver than "code, questionnaire, audit"', says InterfaceFLOR's Ramon Arratia.

Purchasing services rather than products

There is an old cliché that someone buying a hand drill doesn't need the drill, just the holes. Similarly, Xerox would rather not sell you a photocopier. After all, why do you want to own a big lump of beige metal and plastic? No, you want copies of documents, and that is what Xerox wants to sell you instead.

For example, instead of selling solvents, a Chemical Management Services (CMS) company will sell you a solvent service. It will provide the solvent along with any necessary equipment, advise on how it should be used, recover the solvent after use and recycle it for the next use. It is in the provider's interest to minimise wastage of solvent and maximise recovery, so there is a clear environmental benefit. For example, by purchasing a paint CMS, Raytheon reported a 30–40% net reduction in chemical purchase and management costs and a reduction in paint waste of 71%.[41]

Buying such a 'product service system' (PSS) makes a lot of sense in many cases. It sidesteps the problem of purchase costs versus through-life costs, as there are no purchase costs. However, it may take some work to integrate a service into your operations.

Through-life design

The cheapest place to avoid environmental problems throughout the product lifecycle is to design them out of products and services in the first place. Therefore it follows that the drawing board is a powerful tool in building a sustainable supply chain. 'The product is the lifeblood of companies – focus on the product', is the advice of InterfaceFLOR's Ramon Arratia.

Eco-design techniques can be categorised by the two models of sustainability described in Chapter 2. The following generic eco-efficiency principles can be applied to a design:

- Design to use less material (dematerialisation) – design material out of the product (e.g. use stronger, lighter materials or exploit stronger shapes).

- Use energy efficient components (e.g. motors, lights, integrated circuits) and/or reduce friction, electrical and other forms of resistance (e.g. aerodynamic vehicles).

- Improve the utility of the product either by extending the lifecycle, improving performance or providing multi-functional capability – although this isn't a guarantee that the product will be more eco-efficient in practice as it depends on user choices.

You can apply the eco-system principles to product design as follows:

- All materials are either recycled and recyclable, and/or are natural and capable of being returned to nature as a nutrient (e.g. after composting).

- The product is designed to be easily dismantled into its constituent materials for recovery.

- All the energy consumed over the lifecycle is renewable.

- All toxic materials are designed out of the system from cradle to grave.

For example, when Apple released a new iMac model in 2012, it used 68% less material and generated 67% fewer carbon emissions than earlier generations (eco-efficiency). It now uses PVC-free cables and is free of Brominated Flame Retardants, a PBT chemical (eco-system model), but does not appear more ready for the circular economy than older models.[42]

....

CHAPTER 6

Advanced Techniques: Business Model and Corporate Philosophy

IN THE LAST CHAPTER we looked at how changing the organisation's operations and products/services can reduce supply chain impacts. While these techniques present huge scope to make improvements, they are in turn ultimately constrained by the business model and the overall corporate philosophy of the company. This chapter presents the most powerful options in the toolbox – those that assume that everything is up for negotiation. Clearly, potential risk and reward are very high, which typically means buy-in at boardroom level is a prerequisite of these measures.

Choice editing and deleting products

Retailers often practise 'choice editing' – refusing to stock unsustainable products. For example, you cannot buy a tuna sandwich at the Wildfowl and Wetland Trust Centres, because of the Trust's concerns about the sustainability of tuna fishing. At Greggs you can only buy fair trade coffee, tea, sugar and chocolate. B&Q famously refused to stock patio heaters as they did not fit with its sustainability ambitions. Limiting the choice of the consumer to products with a sustainable provenance is a powerful technique, but it requires buy-in throughout the organisation due to the commercial risks involved.

For product manufacturers, the nuclear option is to get rid of products that will never comply with your supply chain ambitions. This takes even more bravery than choice editing, but sustainability leaders like InterfaceFLOR take some relish in deleting profitable product lines that do not comply with their sustainability ambitions, for example, carpets that require toxic flame-retardants.

Selling services rather than products

In the last chapter we looked at buying a service rather than a product – a concept known as a product-service system (PSS), but obviously an option is to sell services rather than a product. The environmental benefits of a PSS flow from the fact that it is in the interest of the customer and provider to minimise the amount of energy and material consumed in delivering the service. This reduction in material/energy requirements usually means fewer resources are required from the supply chain.

Product-service systems are springing up all over the economy, most strikingly Rolls Royce starting to provide a jet engine service rather than selling engines to airlines.[43] However, some offerings, for example, InterfaceFLOR's Evergreen floor covering service and Airworks compressed air service, have failed to take off in the same way.[44] The crucial issue is to determine whether customers are prepared to see the service as a revenue item rather than the traditional capital item.

Shifting to digital services

A shift from physical to digital services replaces physical 'stuff' with data. For example, instead of buying a DVD whose physical form and packaging will clutter up my living room for years to come, I can watch the movie on demand via my cable TV provider or one of the growing numbers of online providers. This means I get the movie I want to watch, but I don't get all the plastics and paper that used to come with it. The digital version also takes much less energy to distribute.

Some industries are going digital fast – music, movies, books, newspapers, magazines and catalogues are all increasingly being dominated by digital products. By making this shift, they are significantly cutting the impacts of their supply chain.

Investing in the supply chain

So far we have assumed that the relationship between suppliers and purchasers is largely transactional. However, some cutting-edge businesses are going far beyond that traditional relationship and actively intervening in the supply chain.

Creating Shared Value (CSV), the brainchild of business gurus Michael Porter and Mark Kramer, is the concept of going beyond Corporate Social Responsibility (CSR) and actively investing in the business eco-system around your organisation for the benefit of all.[45] For example, if Nike promotes active lifestyles then society benefits from better public health, and the market for sportswear grows which in turn benefits Nike.

The CSV concept also applies down the supply chain. For example, Marks & Spencer went into collaboration with one of their lingerie suppliers in Sri Lanka to design and build an 'eco-factory' that requires only 4% of the energy of a traditional factory. The use of natural light and ventilation makes working conditions as far from a sweatshop as could be imagined.

Another example is Google's investment in developing renewable energy technologies.[46] This investment is intended to develop future low carbon energy supplies both for Google itself and others, shaping future supply chains.

Building a new supply chain

But what if there is no viable supply chain for the materials and/or products you need? This is a classic chicken-and-egg situation – until there is demand, there is no supply chain, but without the supply chain, how can you simply create demand? While forward commitment procurement may help (see Chapter 4), it may not create enough demand to stimulate a new supply chain. So how can you generate that demand?

Demand can be stimulated internally. For example, Marks & Spencer has been developing product lines manufactured from recycled polyester including school uniforms, umbrellas and men's suits. However, when they started, there was no viable supply chain for high-grade recycled polyester. The company brought economies of scale to the collection, sorting and processing links in the polyester loop by purchasing a large amount of low grade recycled fibre for uses such as filling cushions. This demand also brought down the cost of high grade recycled polyester fibre. Marks & Spencer hopes that the recycled fibre can soon be produced at a price that is competitive with virgin fibre.

Boosting demand can also be achieved through partnerships. For example, in order to create sufficient demand for hydrogen-powered delivery vans, the European postal services combined forces via the PostEurop organisation. By using forward commitment procurement (see Chapter 4) and some hard bargaining, PostEurop believes it has brought forward the commercialisation of hydrogen technology by a decade – to 2014.

Conclusions

THE DAYS OF AN ORGANISATION drawing the limits of their responsibility around the factory fence or the curtilage of the office block are long gone. For most organisations, the bulk of their environmental footprint is in their supply chain and stakeholders will expect them to take responsibility for that entire footprint.

Unfortunately, of all aspects of organisational sustainability, dealing with the supply chain is the most difficult given the sheer number of issues to be dealt with and the fact they are out of the direct control of the organisation concerned. This short book has been written to make that challenge a little more manageable.

Challenges are fun, however, and while winning the 'hard yards' of green procurement we have described in Chapters 3 and 4 can be a little managerial at times, the more adventurous solutions proposed in Chapters 5 and 6 require creativity and risk-taking. This is truly the buccaneering end of the sustainability profession and should be relished as such.

If I could offer five last pieces of advice they would be:

- Make sure you are dealing with the big issues in your supply chain – nobody will thank you for tinkering around the edges.

- Be ambitious. Incremental targets lead only to incremental improvements; stretch targets lead to breakthrough solutions.

- You won't solve these problems on your own: bring everybody concerned with an issue on board, get them thinking in the right direction and ask for their help in generating solutions.

- Be prepared to get tough. If a supplier won't play ball, find another supplier.

- Relish the challenge. If you're not failing, you're not trying hard enough. Perseverance is the key to success.

It is always worth remembering that every positive change you make in your supply chain, no matter how small, is ultimately a step forwards to a green economy for everyone. That's a noble cause and I wish you every success!

....

Notes and References

1. Fried, I. 2005. Jobs defends Apple's record on environment. *CNET News*, 21 April. Available at: http://news.cnet.com/Jobs-defends-Apples-record-on-environment/2100-1041_3-5680152.html

2. DEFRA. 2012. Leading businesses to disclose greenhouse gas emissions. Press release, 20 June. Available at: https://www.gov.uk/government/news/leading-businesses-to-disclose-greenhouse-gas-emissions

3. Source data for this graph taken from the *Financial Times* and smoothed: http://www.ft.com

4. *Bloomberg News*. 2013. IEA's Birol says oil prices still too high for economic recovery. *Bloomberg News*, 11 September. Available at: http://www.bloomberg.com/news/2013-09-11/iea-s-birol-says-oil-prices-still-too-high-for-economic-recovery.html

5. MGI Commodity Index data sourced from 'Resource revolution: Tracking global commodity markets', McKinsey Global Institute, September 2013.

6. *BusinessGreen*. 2013. Business leaders urge resource scarcity review. *BusinessGreen*, 12 July. Available at: http://www.businessgreen.com/bg/news/2281127/business-leaders-urge-resource-scarcity-review

7. Connor, S. 2009. Warning: Oil supplies are running out fast. *The Independent*, 3 August. Available at: http://www.independent.co.uk/news/science/warning-oil-supplies-are-running-out-fast-1766585.html

8. Congressional Research Service. 2012. 'Rare Earth Elements: The Global Supply Chain', 8 June. Available at: http://www.fas.org/sgp/crs/natsec/R41347.pdf

9. EEF Executive Survey. 2012. Available at: http://www.eef.org.uk/blog/file.axd?file=2012%2F1%2FExecutive+Survey+2012.pdf

10. http://www.theregister.co.uk/2011/09/01/apple_environment_report/

11. 'Emerging potential applications of glycerol are expected to solve its price erosion issues – market insights'. Available at: http://www.europlat.org/emerging-potential-applications-of-glycerol-are-expected-to-solve-its-price-erosion-issues-market-insights.htm

12. Data taken from 'Canon Sustainability Report 2009'. Available at: www.canon.com/environment/report/pdf/report2009e.pdf; 'NHS England carbon footprint: GHG emissions, 1990–2020 baseline emissions update', National Health Service Sustainable Development Unit. Available at: www.sdu.nhs.uk/page.php?page_id=160; Unilever Sustainable Living Plan. Available at: http://www.unilever.com/images/UnileverSustainableLivingPlan_tcm13-284876.pdf; and Apple and the Environment. Available at: http://www.apple.com/uk/environment/our-footprint/

13. Jackson, T. 1996. *Material Concerns: Pollution, Profit and Quality of Life* (Abingdon: Routledge).

14. Royal Society. 2010. 'Climate change: A summary of the science.' Available at: http://royalsociety.org/uploadedFiles/Royal_Society_Content/policy/publications/2010/4294972962.pdf

15. The 2°C Target: Information reference document: Background on impacts emission pathways mitigation options and costs. Prepared and adopted by the EU climate change expert group 'EG Science', 9 July 2008.

16. Benton, D. and Hazell, J. 2013. 'Resource Resilient UK: A Report from the Circular Economy Task Force', Green Alliance.

17. Carson, R. 2000. *Silent Spring* (London: Penguin Classics).

18. FAO. 2012. 'State of the World's Forests', Forestry and Agriculture Organisation of the United Nations. Available at: http://www.fao.org/docrep/016/i3010e/i3010e01.pdf

19. IUCN, Species Extinction – The Facts, The International Union for Conservation

of Nature (IUCN). Available at: http://cmsdata.iucn.org/downloads/species_extinction_05_2007.pdf

20. NASA. 2013. Ozone hole watch. Available at: http://ozonewatch.gsfc.nasa.gov

21. Eurasia Review. 2011. Arctic on verge of record ozone loss. Available at: http://www.eurasiareview.com/25032011-arctic-on-verge-of-record-ozone-loss/

22. Berners-Lee, M. and Clark, D. 2013. *The Burning Question* (London: ProfileBooks), p. 47.

23. Global Reporting Initiative. Available at: https://www.globalreporting.org/

24. Pearce, F. 2013. Cleaning up. *Sunday Telegraph magazine*, 21 July.

25. BSI (2010) BS 8903:2010 Principles and Framework for Procuring Sustainably. British Standards Institute.

26. Kane, G. 2012. *Green Jujitsu: The Smart Way to Embed Sustainability into Your Organisation* (Oxford: Dō Sustainability).

27. Volvo. 2013. Core values requirements on suppliers 2013. Available at: http://www.volvologistics.com/logistics/global/en-gb/about%20us/core%20values/pages/demandsOnCarriers.aspx

28. OSPAR. 1984. Declaration of the International Conference on the Protection of the North Sea. Available at: http://www.ospar.org/html_documents/ospar/html/1nsc-1984-bremen_declaration.pdf

29. These examples were adapted from the British Council's Supplier Evaluation Questionnaire. Available at: http://www.britishcouncil.org%2Fafrica-zm-environmental-supplier-evaluation-questionnaire.doc

30. Apple. 2013. Supplier Responsibility Progress Report 2013. Available at: http://www.apple.com/uk/supplierresponsibility/reports.html

31. Sharp Green Procurement Guidelines. Available at: http://sharp-world.com/corporate/eco/supplier/g_procure/index.html

32. APP. 2013. 'Asia Pulp and Paper's No Deforestation policy continues as it issues its third Sustainability Roadmap "Vision 2020" update'. Press release, 4 June. Available at: http://www.asiapulppaper.com/news-media/press-releases/asia-pulp-and-papers-no-deforestation-policy-continues-it-issues-its-third

33. Example taken from BS 903:2010 Principles and Framework for Procuring Sustainably, British Standards Institute.

34. Pearce, F. 2013. Cleaning up. *Sunday Telegraph magazine*, 21 July.

35. Envirowise. 2006. Cut waste and build profit.

36. Whyles, G. 2012. An integrated ultra low carbon energy solution for NUH: A new procurement approach. Available at: http://www.nuh.nhs.uk/media/917661/A%20New%20Procurement%20Approach.pdf

37. FCP Demonstration Project: HM Prison Service Zero Waste Prison Mattress System. Available at: http://www.sustainable-procurement.org/fileadmin/template/scripts/sp_resources/_tools/put_file.php?uid=8dba396b

38. Diagram based on information from the Kalundborg Symbiosis Institution. Available at: http://www.symbiosis.dk/

39. Reverse logistics for plasterboard: A unique operation to manage the delivery of plasterboard and backhaul the off-cuts and wastage. WRAP. Available at: http://www.wrap.org.uk/sites/files/wrap/Reverse%20Logistics%20-%20Plasterboard.pdf

40. CCC Newsdesk. 2007. The climate change dividend – cutting carbon and saving money. Climate Change Corp, 13 March. Available at: http://www.climatechangecorp.com/content.asp?ContentID=4801 (accessed 28 September 2010).

41. Raytheon: A Chemical Management Services Case Study, Chemical Strategies Partnership. Available at: http://www.chemicalstrategies.org/pdf/case_studies/raytheon_case_study_full.pdf

42. Apple: Environmental Progress. Available at: http://www.apple.com/environment/progress/

43. Baines, T.S. et al. 2007. State-of-the-art in product service-systems. *Proc. IMechE Vol. 221 Part B: J. Engineering Manufacture*. Available at: **http://bura.brunel. ac.uk/bitstream/2438/3812/1/Servitization%20paper%20JEM_858.pdf**

44. Reason, P. et al. 2008. Insider voices: Human dimensions of low carbon technology. Available at: **www.bath.ac.uk/management/news_events/pdf/ lowcarbon_insider_voices.pdf**

45. Porter, M. and Kramer, M. 2011. Creating shared value. *Harvard Business Review* (Vol. 89 Issue 1/2): 62–77.

46. Google: Investing in a Clean Energy Future. Available at: **http://www.google. com/green/energy/investments/**

Lightning Source UK Ltd.
Milton Keynes UK
UKOW04f0432180315

248079UK00002B/42/P